STARS OF SPORTS

KYLIAN MBAPPÉ

SOCCER ICON

■■■ by Ryan G. Van Cleave

CAPSTONE PRESS
a capstone imprint

Published by Capstone Press, an imprint of Capstone
1710 Roe Crest Drive, North Mankato, Minnesota 56003
capstonepub.com

Library of Congress Cataloging-in-Publication Data
Names: Van Cleave, Ryan G., 1972- author. Title: Kylian Mbappé : soccer icon / by Ryan G. Van Cleave.
Description: North Mankato, MN : Capstone Press, [2025] | Series: Sports illustrated kids stars of sports | Includes
bibliographical references and index. | Audience: Ages 8 to 11 | Audience: Grades 4-6 | Summary: "At 7 years old,
Kylian Mbappé scored his first goal. At 16 years old, he made his professional soccer debut. At 19, he helped France win
a World Cup. Every year after that brought more fame and success for Mbappé. Learn all about this unstoppable soccer
superstar and how he has changed the game in this enlightening biography"—Provided by publisher. Identifiers: LCCN
2023054400 (print) | LCCN 2023054401 (ebook) | ISBN 9781669076520 (hardcover) | ISBN 9781669076681 (paperback)
ISBN 9781669076698 (pdf) | ISBN 9781669076711 (kindle edition) | ISBN 9781669076704 (epub) Subjects: LCSH:
Mbappé, Kylian, 1988—Juvenile literature. | Soccer players—France—Biography—Juvenile literature. Classification:
LCC GV942.7.M3928 V36 2025 (print) | LCC GV942.7.M3928 (ebook) | DDC 796.334092 [B]—dc23/eng/20231130
LC record available at https://lccn.loc.gov/2023054400
LC ebook record available at https://lccn.loc.gov/2023054401

Editorial Credits
Editor: Christianne Jones; Designer: Jaime Willems; Media Researchers: Jo Miller and Svetlana Zhurkin;
Production Specialist: Whitney Shaefer

Image Credits
Alamy: Abaca Press/Henri Szwarc, 7, Abaca Press/Jerome Domine, 21, Abaca Press/Laurent Zabulon, 19, DPPI Media/
Stephane Allman, 5, Xinhua/Cao Can, 15; Associated Press: Thibault Camus, cover, 8; Getty Images: Oisin Keniry,
25; Newscom: MAXPPP/Leon Tanguy, 13, Xinhua News Agency/Gao Jing, 23, ZUMA Press/Panoramic, 10, 27, 28;
Shutterstock: August_0802, 17, Christian Bertrand, 26, EFKS, 1, Influential Photography, 11, Victor Velter, 16

Source Notes
Page 9, "Kylian would always think about football . . ." John Bennett, "Kylian Mbappé: How France World Cup star rose to
prominence," BBV World Service Sport, June 30, 2018, www.bbc.co.uk/sport/football/44669497, Accessed June 2023.

Page 9, "I'm going to play. . ." Jeremy Patrelle, "10 things we learned about Kylian Mbappé in the L'Quipe documentary,"
GQ France, November 7, 2017, www.gqmagazine.fr/lifestyle/sport/articles/10-trucs-que-lon-a-appris-sur-kylian-mbappe-
dans-le-docu-kylian-hors-normes-de-lequipe-enquete/57616, Accessed June 2023.

Page 12, "It was hard for me to be . . ." "Kylian Mbappé: Paris St-Germain forward wants his charity to help kids live their
dream," BBC, January 22, 2020, www.bbc.co.uk/newsround/51187358, Accessed June 2023.

Page 18, "We will return . . ." Sam Blitz, "Kylian Mbappé: France star well-laced to become the best player on the planet
after World Cup heroics," Sky Sports, December 20, 2023, www.skysports.com/football/news/11095/12771383/kylian-
mbappe-france-star-well-placed-to-become-the-best-player-on-the-planet-after-world-cup-final-heroics, Accessed June
2023.

Page 22, "It doesn't change my life . . ." Ken Browne, "Kylian Mbappé: 12 things you may not know about France's football
star," Olympics.com, April 25, 2023, https://olympics.com/en/news/kylian-mbappe-tokyo-olympics-12-fun-facts, Accessed
June 2023.

Page 27, "Mbappé is the future and the present . . ." The Esquire Editors, "What Football Legends Have to Say About Kylian
Mbappé," Esquire, June 2, 2021, www.esquire.com/uk/culture/a36600159/what-football-legends-have-to-say-about-kylian-
mbappe, Accessed June 2023.

Page 28, "I am aware of the risk. . ." Jason Burt, "Grounded Kylian Mbappe will go all the way to the very top of the game,"
The Telegraph, July 2, 2018, www.telegraph.co.uk/world-cup/2018/07/02/grounded-kylian-mbappe-will-go-way-top-
game, Accessed June 2023.

Printed and bound in the USA. PO 5853

TABLE OF CONTENTS

Words in **BOLD** are in the glossary.

WORLD CUP DREAMS COME TRUE

At 19, Kylian Mbappé was playing for the French national team in the biggest soccer tournament in the world. This was the 2018 FIFA World Cup in Moscow, Russia. The tournament is played every four years.

The score was 0–0 despite both teams launching shot after shot. Then 34 minutes into the game, a French teammate **dribbled** up and tried to score. The shot was **deflected**. Mbappé saw his chance. He charged in and smashed the ball into the net.

GOAL!

The crowd went wild! Mbappé became the youngest player to score in a World Cup final. His goal helped France move ahead in the tournament. The team went on to win the World Cup.

Signature Celebration

Mbappé has a unique celebration after he scores. He crosses his arms and wedges his hands into his armpits. This celebration goes back to his childhood. His brother Ethan did it after beating Mbappé at a soccer video game.

CHAPTER ONE

A STAR IN THE MAKING

Kylian Mbappé Lottin was born in Paris, France, on December 20, 1998. He grew up in Bondy, a suburb of Paris. His father, Wilfried, was a soccer player and coach. His mother, Fayza, was a former professional handball player. They created a supportive and sports-loving environment for Mbappé and his two brothers.

All three boys loved soccer from the start. Mbappé's adopted older brother, Jirès Kembo Ekoko, was already playing soccer at a high level. Mbappé and his younger brother, Ethan, showed exceptional ability too.

Because their father was first a player and later a coach, the boys grew up around soccer. Mbappé followed his father everywhere. He participated in training sessions when he was just 3 years old.

⟩⟩⟩ Fayza, Ethan, and Wilfried Mbappé
waiting for a soccer match in 2017.

At 6, Mbappé joined AS Bondy. It was his local soccer team. His father was the coach. Mbappé's speed and ability to score goals set him apart. He quickly became a standout player.

〉〉〉 AS Bondy players (green uniforms) compete in a match.

Antonio Riccardi, who coached the AS Bondy under-13 team, said, "Kylian would always think about football [soccer], always talk about football, always watch football—and if he wasn't doing that he'd be playing football games on the PlayStation."

Mbappé also played soccer with his friends in the Bondy streets. He couldn't get enough! He had big dreams of becoming a professional soccer player. "I'm going to play on the French team," he told everyone. "I'm going to play in the World Cup with France."

Some people laughed when he said that. They weren't laughing for long.

FACT

Between the ages of 6 and 11, Mbappé studied music at a center for the performing arts. He learned to sing and play the flute.

CHAPTER TWO

RISING THROUGH THE RANKS

Mbappé continued to wow coaches, crowds, and **opponents**. In 2011, he enrolled at the INF Clairefontaine. It was a special school for top soccer players.

In 2013, 14-year-old Mbappé joined the AS Monaco youth academy. He continued to develop his soccer skills.

〉〉〉 Mbappé playing for AS Monaco

>>> Mbappé plays in a 2017 game in Paris.

FACT

Mbappé's father retired from coaching to help manage his son's career. He is his **agent**.

Two years later, he made his professional **debut** with the club. With his help, AS Monaco won the French Ligue 1 title in the 2016–2017 season. His performance on the field didn't go unnoticed. Mbappé received the Golden Boy award in 2017 as the best under-21 player in Europe.

Mbappé's dazzling play also drew the attention of Paris Saint-Germain (PSG). It is one of the top soccer clubs in Europe. They immediately signed him to a $195 million deal. This made him the highest-paid teenage player ever. As a member of PSG, Mbappé continued his path to greatness.

"It was hard for me to be famous very young," he said. As always, his parents were a great help. "They were there for me and they say stay calm, stay with your values."

FACT

In addition to his native language of French, Mbappé speaks English and Spanish fluently. He speaks some Portuguese and Italian as well.

>>> Mbappé takes photos with his family after being presented with his PSG jersey in 2017.

CHAPTER THREE

SUPERSTAR SUCCESS

Mbappé's success with PSG soon translated to the international stage. In 2018, he was chosen to represent France in the FIFA World Cup in Russia. This selection was a huge honor.

Despite being only 19, Mbappé scored four goals. One took place during the final match against Croatia. Not only did he help France win their second-ever World Cup, but he also won the FIFA World Cup Best Young Player award.

From his earliest years, Mbappé wanted to do more and push limits. So it was no surprise when he said, "It was not the end when I won the World Cup. It was the first chapter of something crazy."

>>> Mbappé holds up the World Cup
Best Young Player award.

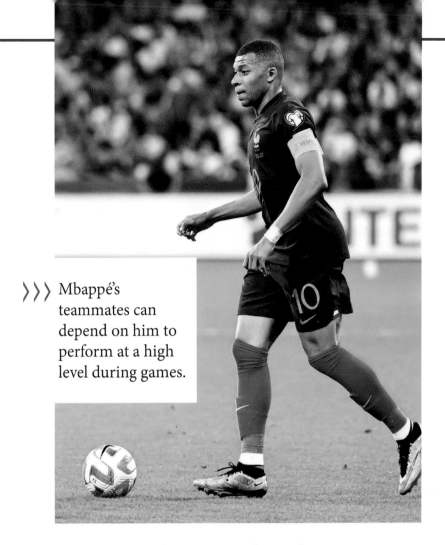

>>> Mbappé's teammates can depend on him to perform at a high level during games.

Over the next few years, Mbappé's success was amazing. He became the top goal scorer 10 times, with his highest goal count reaching 29. He also became the French Footballer of the Year three times. His amazing performance helped PSG become French champions six times and win the French Cup three times. He won the Player of the Year award four seasons in row.

This success paid off. Mbappé earned a new three-year deal worth more than $263 million. It made him the highest-paid soccer player in the world.

When it was time for the 2022 World Cup, everyone had the same question: Would Mbappé lead France to back-to-back World Cup victories?

FACT

Mbappé has a well-known sneaker obsession. It began with a pair of Nike Air Max 1 sneakers.

AIR MAX 1

Mbappé started strong. He fired off five goals in the matches leading up to the finals. But France's opponent, Argentina, had its own superstar. This superstar was Lionel Messi.

In what many call the greatest World Cup match ever, the lead went back and forth. Mbappé scored three goals, but the score was 3–3 at the end of **regulation**. In the penalty kick **shoot-out**, Argentina won 4–2.

Soon after that disappointing loss, Mbappé shifted his focus to the 2026 World Cup. "We will return," he tweeted.

So Many Options

Mbappé could have played for three different teams in the World Cup. His mother is Algerian. His father is from Cameroon. He was born in France. His loyalty remained with the place he was born and raised—France.

>>> Mbappé and his team faced superstar Lionel Messi at the 2022 World Cup.

CHAPTER FOUR

A WINNER ON AND OFF THE FIELD

Mbappé is admired for his skills on the field, which include more than his physical movements. He is admired for his exceptional sportsmanship. He always supports his teammates. He celebrates all of their victories. He encourages them during challenging times.

But it's not just his own team that he respects. Mbappé has **consoled** opponents after tough games too. He shows that true sportsmanship is more than winning or losing.

Mbappé understands that the power of sports can change lives. He uses his platform to make a positive impact wherever he can. He works with organizations like Premiers de Cordée. This organization coordinates sports activities for children with disabilities.

>>> Mbappé and his brother Ethan work with children at a Premiers de Cordée event.

Mbappé donated his 2018 World Cup earnings to a charity for children with disabilities. The amount was around $500,000. "It doesn't change my life, but it changes theirs," he said. "And if it can change theirs, it is a great pleasure."

In 2020, Mbappé launched Inspired by Kylian Mbappé (IBKM). This organization helps children achieve their dreams. How? By supporting them in whatever career path they choose.

His big heart extends to animals as well. In 2021, Mbappé and Chinese Olympic diving gold medalist Zhang Jiaqi became the godparents of twin pandas. The pandas were born at a zoo in France. The athletes hope to create awareness about endangered species.

FACT

In 2022, Mbappé launched Zebra Valley. This Los Angeles-based entertainment company creates cross-platform content to encourage global diversity.

>>> Zhang Jiaqi and Mbappé pose with the twin panda cubs in 2021.

CHAPTER FIVE

THE BRIGHT FUTURE AHEAD

Mbappé's story is one of determination, talent, and hard work. It's a reminder that success is not only measured by trophies and praise. It's also measured by the positive impact one can have on others.

Mbappé has already scored big in the world of soccer, and he's just getting started. Before turning 20, he was a global **icon**. He graced the cover of the video game *FIFA 2021*. That was a dream come true for a guy who loves the game.

So what's next for the soccer icon? Maybe another World Cup or two. But first, he is going to play for a new team. As a child, Mbappé loved Real Madrid. In early 2024, he signed a contract to join the team.

>>> Mbappé inspires others with his determination and skills.

Mbappé also dreams of winning the Ballon d'Or award for the world's best soccer player. It's one of the few awards he hasn't won yet.

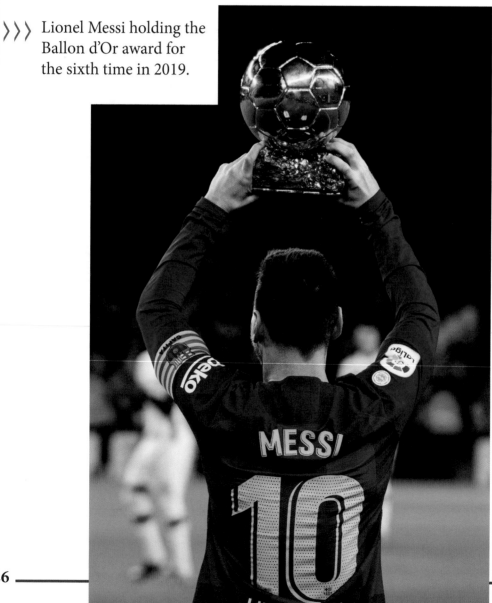

〉〉〉 Lionel Messi holding the Ballon d'Or award for the sixth time in 2019.

>>> Cristiano Ronaldo and Mbappé greet each other on the field in France.

Perhaps the most meaningful praise came from his childhood hero, soccer legend Cristiano Ronaldo. "Mbappé is the future and the present."

⟩⟩⟩ Mbappé enjoys spending time with fans.

Through it all, Mbappé stays humble. "I am aware of the risk with all the media attention, all the glitz and glamour around football," Mbappé said. "I know where I come from."

No matter where he goes or what he does, one thing is clear. As long as Mbappé stays true to himself and never loses sight of his roots, the future will remain as bright as his contagious smile.

TIMELINE

1998   Born in Paris, France, on December 20

2004   Joins AS Bondy youth soccer team and was coached by his father

2011   Attends the prestigious Clairefontaine academy to train among top French soccer talent

2013   Joins AS Monaco youth academy, officially becoming a professional soccer player

2015   Makes professional soccer debut for AS Monaco

2017   Wins Ligue 1 title with AS Monaco

2017   Transfers to Paris Saint-Germain (PSG)

2018   Wins FIFA World Cup with the French team; becomes youngest player to score in a World Cup final since Pelé

2018   Awarded the Legion of Honor with his team, France's highest order of merit

2020   Launches Inspired by Kylian Mbappé (IBKM)

2021   Wins UEFA Nations League; France becomes first nation to win this award, a World Cup, and a Europea Championship

2021   Featured on cover of the video game *FIFA 2021*

2023   Named one of *Time* magazine's 100 Most Influential People in the World

2024   Signs contract with Real Madrid

GLOSSARY

AGENT (AY-juhnt)—a person authorized to act on another's behalf

CONSOLE (kuhn-SOHL)—comfort

DEBUT (DAY-byoo)—first appearance or performance

DEFLECT (dih-FLEKT)—bounce off

DRIBBLE (DRIH-buhl)—to move the ball along the ground with the feet

ICON (AHY-kon)—a person admired for having great influence on something

OPPONENT (uh-POH-nuhnt)—a person who competes against another person

REGULATION (reh-gyuh-LAY-shuhn)—the normal period of time that a game is played

SHOOT-OUT (SHOOT-owt)—a method used to determine the winner of a game tied after regulation play and overtime; players from each team take turns trying to score goals from the penalty spot

READ MORE

Ashby, Kevin, and Michael Part. *Kylian Mbappé: The Golden Boy*. Beverly Hills, CA: Sole Books, 2021.

Jökulsson, Illugi. *Stars of World Soccer: Fourth Edition*. New York: Abbeville Press, 2023.

Tran, Kerry. *The Mbappé Effect: How Kylian is Redefining Football's Limits*. Independently published, 2023.

INTERNET SITES

ESPN—Kylian Mbappé
espn.com/soccer/player/_/id/231388/kylian-mbappe

Kylian Mbappé: News
kylianmbappe.com/en/news

Paris Saint-Germain Official Website—Kylian Mbappé
en.psg.fr/teams/first-team/squad/kylian-mbappe

INDEX

AUTHOR BIO

Ryan G. Van Cleave is the author of dozens of books for children and hundreds of articles published in magazines. As The Picture Book Whisperer, they help celebrities write books for children. Ryan lives in Florida.